The Original Ending of the Gospel of Mark 16:1-8

Terry Kwanghyun Eum

CreateSpace
North Charleston, SC

© 2015 Terry Kwanghyun Eum

The Original Ending of the Gospel of Mark 16:1-8

North Charleston, South Carolina

ISBN-13: 978-1517510312
ISBN-10: 1517510317

For

ἡ βασιλεία τοῦ θεου

My Beloved Professor, Rev. Dr. Frances Taylor Gench

My Beloved Wife, Chelsea I. Eum

1st Son, Isaac S. Eum

2nd Son, Caleb Y. Eum

3rd Son, Enoch H. Eum

Acknowledgement

When I was a seminary student at Union Presbyterian Seminary, Dr. Frances Taylor Gench encouraged me, helped me, taught me, and guided me to be where I am at today. She encouraged me to wrestle with the Scripture, she pushed me to dig deeper, she gave opportunities to study and meditate the Scriptures academically.

The Gospel of Mark is my personal favorite Gospel in the Bible, also my area of concentrated study in the New Testament. The ending of the Gospel of Mark was my Th.M. thesis.

As I publish this book, I'd like to express my love and gratitude to my beloved professor Frances Taylor Gench, without her, I would not be the same person. Also I'd like to express my love and gratitude to my beloved wife, Chelsea I. Eum who raises our three gifts from God Isaac, Caleb, and Enoch faithfully, lovingly, and beautifully. Through her supports, love, and encouragements, I am doing the ministry of God for ἡ βασιλεία τοῦ θεου ("*the reign/kingdom of God*").

The Original Ending of the Gospel of Mark is waiting for the readers to respond to the message of the resurrection of Jesus. May this book enlighten you what our God through the ending of the Gospel of Mark is trying to tell you.

Terry Kwanghyun Eum
Richmond, Virginia

Contents

Introduction

The enigmatic final scene in Mark's Gospel (Mark 16:1-8) has evoked a great deal of scholarly debate, for at first glance, it appears to be an odd way to conclude a Gospel: *"So they went out and fled from the tomb, for terror and amazement had seized them; and they said nothing to anyone, for they were afraid"* (16:8). The text displays the failures of the world, humankind, including the disciples, and even the faithful women followers of Jesus. The author of the Gospel of Mark incorporates the traditions into the empty tomb narrative for his own community. While scholars have debated whether or not the evangelist intended to end the Gospel at this point, I am convinced that it is the original and intended ending. The text boldly conveys that the events surrounding the empty tomb are in God's hands, and this text shows that God is the one who is leading and in charge of the event of the empty tomb. The absence of a narrative of appearances of the risen Jesus places more emphasis on the mysterious activity of God in the resurrection than Jesus Christ, the Son of God. God is working throughout the narrative, and is working on the restoration and the reconciliation of His people, even Peter. The readers and the audiences of the text are to follow Jesus, who goes before us, and make journeys to Galilee.

This book will pay special attention to a cultural dimension of the text and its bearing on interpretation. The text is written in the honor and shame culture that existed in the Mediterranean world. According to Richard L. Rohribaugh, "*Notions about honor and shame exist in virtually all cultures. But in many Western societies these terms play a minor role in descriptions of prominent social*

values. Indeed, many people today regard 'honor' as an old-fashioned word, while we normally associate the term 'shame' with the most private aspects of our lives. In both past and present Mediterranean societies, however, honor and shame have played a dominant role in public life."[1]
The philosophers and the Jews, the pagans and the Christians all regarded honor and shame as their primary axis of value. According to David A. deSilva, "*Those living or reared in Asiatic, Latin American, Mediterranean or Islamic countries have considerable advantage in their reading of the New Testament in this regard, since many of those cultures place a prominent emphasis on honor and shame. Readers living in the United States or Western Europe may recognize immediately that we live at some distance from the honor culture of the first-century Greco-*

---

[1] Richard L. Rohrbaugh., *The Social Sciences and New Testament Interpretation* (Grand Rapids, MI: Baker Academic, 1996), 19.

Roman world."[2] DeSilva's observation struck a chord with me. I was born in South Korea and spent my childhood there, and over the last 16 years have assumed Korean-American identity. As a bi-cultural reader of Mark's Gospel, I instinctively bring an awareness of honor and shame dynamics to my reading of biblical texts, as they are values embedded in my cultural context. As I read the concluding scene of the Gospel of Mark, I will also bring other insights from my cultural context to bear on my interpretation of it. As I was educated in an American context, I find myself in a position to "*bridge*" cultures, to bring western perspectives into conversation with Korean culture. I hope my examination of Mark 16:1-8 from my bi-cultural social location might provide new insights for Korean and Korean American faith communities as they engage its witness to the power of God.

---

[2] David A. deSILVA., *Honor, Patronage, Kinship & Purity: Unlocking New Testament Culture* (Downers Grove, IL: InterVarsity Press, 2000), 25.

The Cultural World of the NT

Before delving into the text, it is important to summarize scholarly insights about aspects of life in the first-century world that bear on a reading of it. Honor and shame were pivotal values in antiquity that structured the daily lives of peoples around the Mediterranean, including Jesus and his disciples.

First of all, living conditions in the first-century Mediterranean world were very different from today's living conditions. A study shows that many people died before they reached their first birthday. About one-third of those who survived the first year of life were dead by age six. Nearly sixty percent of these survivors died by age sixteen. By age twenty-six, seventy-five percent were dead; and by age forty-six, ninety percent were deceased. Less

than three percent of the population made it to age sixty.[3]
Conditions were even more dire for those among the
peasant population, which included most biblical characters
and Jesus himself. One-fourth of a Palestinian peasant's
one thousand eight hundred calories per day came from
alcohol. At thirty-two or thirty-three years of age, if indeed
he lived that long, Jesus would have been older than
perhaps eighty percent of his contemporaries, who would
have been ridden with disease, malnourished, and looking
at a decade or less of life expectancy. As Douglas
Oakman's study of village life in ancient Palestine has
shown, violence was a regular part of village experience.
Fraud, robbery, forced imprisonment or labor, beatings,
inheritance disputes, and forcible collection of rents were
commonplace. By late in the first century, nearly half the
arable land in the entire region of Galilee had been
accumulated in this way by just three families. In fact, the

---

[3] Rohrbaugh, 5.

entire population of at least one village had become indebted tenants of one of these absentee landlords.[4] This is the context in which Jesus conducted his public ministry. These conditions prevailed in Galilee, where the Gospel of Mark locates that ministry. This is also the area of Galilee where Jesus conducted his public ministry according to the narrative of the Gospel of Mark. Thus Jesus' ministry, teaching and preaching of the Kingdom of God would surely have conveyed hope and healing to his audiences who were living in dire circumstances. Thus many, no doubt, experienced hopeless and fear upon Jesus' death.

Biblical scholars nowadays have grown increasingly aware of the importance of looking at texts not only in their historical or literary or social contexts but also in their cultural contexts.[5] We can fairly say, given our U.S. experience, that the focal institution of American society is

---

[4] Ibid., 6.
[5] deSilva, 17.

economics. Within this framework, the organizing

principle of American life is instrumental mastery – the

individual's ability to control his or her environment,

personal and impersonal, in order to attain quantity-

oriented success: wealth, ownership, "*good looks*," proper

grades, and all other measurable indications of success.[6]

However, the culture of the first-century world was built on

the foundational social values of honor and shame.[7] Thus

as Jesus was gaining popularity with the crowd, he acquired

honor. Also, since Jesus was perceived as an honorable

man, his handpicked disciples would have had honor

ascribed to them as well.

Honor is the general, abstract word for the worth,

value, prestige, and reputation which is attributed to an

individual and acknowledged by others. According to its

---

[6] Bruce J. Malina., *The New Testament World: Insights from Cultural Anthropology* (Louisville, KY: Westminster John Knox Press, 2001), 29.
[7] desilva, 23.

Greek root, "*honor*" (τιμή) refers to the price or value of

something, such as the "*price*" paid as compensation or

satisfaction for an injury or insult. However, "*honor*" has

to do with public value and worth.[8] Honor is

fundamentally the public recognition of one's social

standing. There are two types of honors: ascribed and

acquired. Ascribed honor is inherited from the family at

birth. Generally it comes simply from being born into a

certain family. Male children have more value than female

children in the eyes of parents and neighbors; and the

firstborn male, who is presumably the heir, has more status

than his younger siblings. Moreover, ascribed honor can

come as well from the political institutions of ancient

society. As an example, Pilate's appointment by Caesar

would be considered as a form of ascribed honor.[9] On the

other hand, acquired honor is the socially recognized claim

---

[8] Jerome H. Neyrey., *Honor And Shame in the Gospel of Matthew*
(Louisville, KY: Westminster John Knox Press, 1998), 15.
[9] Ibid., 16.

to worth that a person acquires by excelling over others in social interaction, such as challenge and response.[10]

The opposite of honor is shame. Shame has become something of a buzzword in the contemporary study of psychology. There are at least three kinds of shame. The first is the *"feeling"* or *"experience"* of shame which means the warmth under the skin and extreme self-consciousness that overtakes an individual when he or she has done something that provokes public disapproval or ridicule. The second is a *"sense"* of shame. This is the predilection to avoid certain behaviors that may incur shame. The third kind of shame occasionally reaches the intensity of fully inflamed self-hatred, and is a kind of a shame that drives people toward perfectionism, withdrawal, diffidence, and combativeness.[11] Nevertheless, the simplest definition of shame is to say that it is the opposite of honor, that is, the

---

[10] Malina, 32.
[11] deSilva, 89.

loss of respect, regard, worth, and value in the eyes of others. Synonyms of shame in this sense would be loss of face, disgrace, and dishonor.[12] Shamed individuals in the ancient world were expected to display shyness, not concern for prestige; deference, not concern for precedence; submission, not aggressiveness; timidity, not daring; and restraint, not boldness. These kinds of understandings about honor and shame had significant bearing on broad social expectations about women's conduct in antiquity. That is, they were judged positively in the court of reputation when they lived up to the social expectations encoded in gender stereotypes.[13] Male disciples are conspicuously absent from Mark's final scene, indicating that they were not faithful enough or bold enough to remain with Jesus. In their case, shame would have been associated with this absence; those who had probably been

---

[12] Neyrey, 30.
[13] Ibid., 32.

regarded as honorable individuals prior to this failure

would now be viewed as shamed individuals.

Women's Roles in Funerary Rituals

At first glance, it seems unusual that three women appeared at the crucial points of the end of Mark's narrative: at the crucifixion, the burial, and the empty tomb. Culturally speaking, in the first century Mediterranean world, men occupy the public spaces, while women are generally directed toward the private spaces of home and hearth. A woman could be seen in the company of her husband, but was to stay hidden at home when he was away.[14] In the Gospels we find the two brothers, Peter and Andrew, sharing a house and a business, as do Zebedee and his two sons (the presence of hired servants suggests a rather successful trade, too). Their wives might participate in this business by preparing, salting, or drying the fish, while also engaging in traditional *"women's work"*

---

[14] deSilva, 33.

involving textiles. Jewish women appear to have had great dealings in public. For example, not only did they go to wells, but markets too. Later markets and wells were considered part of the *"private"* spaces of women since the women of a village would all meet there early in the morning to draw water for the family use that day.[15] Also, preparations for burial were traditionally carried out by women.[16] Thus the three women in the text may have behaved according to social expectations, at least in their journey to the tomb to anoint the dead body of Jesus.

The portrayal of the women in Mark 16 suggests that women were entrusted with significant roles in the ancient funerary rituals in the Mediterranean world. Since the text was written in the context of the Greco-Roman world for Jewish Christians and Gentile Christians, it is

---

[15] deSilva, 183.

[16] D.A. Carson, R.T. France, J.A. Motyer, G.J. Wenham., *New Bible Commentary:21st Century Edition* (Nottingham, England: Inter-Varsity Press, 1994), 976.

important to attend to funerary rituals in Greek, Roman,

Jewish, and early Christian cultures.

Greek Funerary Rituals

In ancient Greece, women played a central role in the burial and lamentation of the dead. Care for the dead was a family responsibility.[17] Obviously men performed various tasks too such as washing, anointing and lamenting the dead. Normally women in a family customarily washed and anointed the dead. As they washed and anointed the dead bodies, many women put a coin on the dead, normally in the mouth of the dead to pay the fare for Charon's ferry. In Greek mythology, Charon or Kharon is the ferryman of Hades who carries souls of the newly deceased across the rivers that divided the world of the living from the world of the dead. Even though some men were professional mourners, women mourners were prominent. According to

---

[17] Kathleen E. Corley., *Maranatha: Women's Funerary Rituals and Christian Origins* (Minneapolis, MN: Fortress Press, 2010), 23.

Corley, it seems *"that attitudes about the respectability of masculine grief underwent change in ancient Greece."*[18] Thus men's grief eventually became unacceptable, while women's grief and mourning assumed prominence. However, men are depicted on vase-representations as joining women in funerary dances, and a few vases depict smaller characters, which perhaps suggest that children, too, engaged in traditional mourning postures. Women were to put both hands to their heads and tear their hair, whereas men were to put one hand to the head without tearing the hair.

Additionally, women were normally mourners and flute players. Funerals were often very public affairs which took place during the day light hours. According to Corley, *"Rites at the gravesite that women performed included continued lamentation and calling to the dead, which was accompanied by various offerings (often food) and*

---

[18] Corley, 24.

libations. These rituals, especially the cries and wailings, were thought to raise the spirit of the dead from the grave."[19] Women prepared funerary meals and food, and shared the funerary meals at the gravesites. Eventually, a ritual funerary meal was held in the house of the deceased, probably immediately following the funeral. Later on, women's mourning was viewed as "*uncontrolled*" and "*unmanly,*" whereas restrained expressions of male grief were said to praise the dead. Thus, legislation eventually emerged that restricted various women's funeral practices in the Greek world. However, women continued to visit tombs of nonrelatives with other women and to mourn and take offerings to their dead.[20] It is clear that women played a central role in funerary practices in ancient Greece.

---

[19] Ibid., 25.
[20] Ibid., 27.

Roman Funerary Rituals

Roman burial customs are also worth considering. Indeed, some scholars propose that the evangelist Mark wrote from Rome. While I think this is unlikely, Greco-Roman culture would have influenced burial practices throughout the Roman Empire, including Palestine. Thus I will include Roman burial customs in this survey. Since Greek customs influenced the West, we see some similarities between Roman funerary customs and Greek funerary customs. In both Greek and Roman burial customs, a coin was placed in the mouth of the dead to pay the fare for Charon's ferry, the corpse was washed, anointed, and a wreath was placed around the head.[21] Additionally, women mourned, beat their breasts and also tore their hair like the Greeks.

---

[21] Ibid., 28.

Differences can be noted as well. In Roman funerary rituals, friends and family members usually gathered at the deathbed, and the nearest relative gave the dying his or her last kiss, ostensibly to catch the soul as it left the body with the last breath. According to Corley, *"Catching this last breath was very important to the bereaved, and Cicero reports that mothers even spent the night outside prisons hoping to give their sons this final kiss before their executions. Upon death the eyes and mouth were closed by a close relative, often a woman or mother."*[22] Also in contrast with Greek practices, dead bodies were generally cremated and the ashes kept in urns in the tomb. But for those who were poor, inhumation was fairly common, and eventually the entire Roman Empire took up the practice of inhumation. Romans visited the graves of their family members and held a funerary feast at the tomb on the day of funeral. Women prepared food,

---

[22] Ibid., 28.

visited tombs, and even attended Roman funerary meals.

According to Corley, *"The deceased were thought to be present for these meals, and the mourners set food out for them, even pouring food into the burial site if the meal was being held at the gravesite. Some tombs even had kitchens."*[23] If this was the case, women probably prepared the foods that the deceased once liked when he or she was alive, since Romans believed that the deceased were to be present for the meals. As a Korean American, the Romans' belief of the deceased's presence for the funerary meals struck me, because there is a Korean traditional funerary custom called *"Chesa"*[24] (제사) which contains very similar elements. Even though the *"Chesa"* ritual was one of the most common Confucian rituals to honor deceased ancestors in ancient China,[25] Koreans received the ritual as

---

[23] Ibid., 29.

[24] Nicole Wilkinson Duran, Teresa Okure, Daniel M. Patte., *Mark*, Texts@Contexts (Minneapolis, MN: Fortress Press, 2011), 22.

[25] Kim Chongho., *Korean Shamanism: The Cultural Paradox* (Hants, England: Ashgate, 2003), 42.

they were being influenced by Confucianism from China, and practice of it continues to this day.

In the Korean traditional culture, the eldest son, sometimes the eldest grandson or a male family of the deceased was responsible for providing the "*Chesa*," the Korean traditional funerary ritual. However, even though males were responsible for providing the "*Chesa*," mainly women in the deceased family did the majority of preparation for the "*Chesa*," arranging the funeral, hiring the mourners, and cooking for the funerary meals. They also presented food for the deceased, and usually poured drink that they liked when they were alive on the gravesite, believing that the deceased ate the prepared meals.[26] Normally, after they present the food at the gravesite, they give some time for the deceased to "*eat*" the food. After taking some time off, then those who participate and also those who are around the funerary rituals consume the

---

[26] Duran., 20.

prepared meals. Also, they hold this funerary ritual for the deceased annually. It is very interesting to see similar funerary customs of Rome and Korea. Ancient people probably thought about the deceased in similar ways. Even though women in both Greek and Roman cultures generally held lower status or inferior status compared to men in their societies, they held prominent roles in funerary customs in Roman culture as well as Korean culture.

Jewish Funerary Rituals

Given that Christianity was rooted in the context of Judaism, it is important to look at Jewish funerary rituals. Scholars have long associated the complex rites involved in the *"Cult of the dead"* with non-Israelite religions and cultures, but archaeological evidence indicates that the *"Cult of the dead"* was regularly practiced among Israelites.[27] Even the priestly family of the High Priest Caiaphas used similar practices. One woman in the Caiaphas family, Miriam daughter of Simon, had a coin placed on her tongue for the ferryman Charon.[28] Also, excavations of Jewish tombs displayed perfume bottles, signs of the anointing of remains, dining benches, tables and cups for water for the deceased, as well as cooking pots

---

[27] Corley., 49.
[28] Ibid., 51.

and lamp stands.[29] This suggests that so-called pagan customs persisted among Jews. The "*Cult of the dead*" has a long history in the ancient Near East. Therefore many Jewish men and women probably participated in the "*Cult of the dead*," and also received some of the funerary rituals from the cult. In the Jewish context, Jewish males in Palestine were allowed to prepare only men for burial, but women prepared corpses of either sex. Also, Jewish women could prepare funerary meals or food and drink offerings for the dead. Although both men and women could be professional mourners in the ancient Near East, mourning the dead was more often done by women. Even in the Hebrew Bible women were reciters and probably the composers of traditional laments for the dead. According to Jeremiah 9:17, "*This is what the LORD Almighty says: 'Consider now! Call for the wailing women to come; send for the most skillful of them.'*" Also 2 Chronicles 35:25

---

[29] Ibid., 50.

notes, *"Jeremiah composed laments for Josiah, and to this day all the men and women singers commemorate Josiah in the laments. These became a tradition in Israel and are written in the Laments."* Thus both women and male lamented and mourned in the Jewish context. However, holding the job of professional mourner may not have been very popular for men. According to Carol Meyers, *"In the ancient Near East and Aegean, professional mourners were almost always women; and in Egypt they were exclusively women. Ethnography also indicates that funerary lamentations are typically recited by women, and ancient iconography depicts women in mourning gestures."*[30] Both women and men may have lamented and mourned for the dead, but the Hebrew Bible and archeological evidence suggests that women were more likely professional mourners.

---

[30] Carol A. Newsom, Sharon H. Ringe, Jacqueline E. Lapsley., *Women's Bible Commentary: Twentieth – Anniversary Edition* (Louisville, KY: Westminster John Knox Press, 2012), 359.

Additionally, Jewish women practiced weeping or keening and the singing of formal laments, which were similar to those of neighboring cultures. To have one's death go unsung or unmourned was considered unfortunate. Other customs included fasting, scattering dust, tearing garments, wearing sackcloth, dancing, and funeral feasts that included feeding the dead at tombs.[31] However, just as Greek and Roman legislation emerged which limited women's participation in funerary rituals, rabbis from the second to fourth centuries developed funerary restrictions. They were interested in the control of both funeral expenses as well as women's mourning rituals. Rabbinic literature also shows an increased stress on the impurity caused by death, corpses, and tombs, which also functions to limit the frequency of tomb visitation, especially after the first year.[32] However, the custom of tomb and gravesite

---

[31] Corley., 45.
[32] Ibid., 54.

visitation by women and family lamenting their loved ones and bringing them food and gifts had thousands of years of tradition on its side. There is no doubt that women played prominent roles in funerary rituals, and also led funerary rituals even in Jewish religion.

Christian Funerary Rituals

In sum, women played leading roles in funerary rituals in Greek, Roman, Jewish and even Korean cultures. When we turn to the early Christian context, there is little doubt that women played significant roles in funerary rituals among early Christian groups as well. Early Christians met at tombs and gravesites for funerals of family and friends, but also for the Eucharist. Women participated fully in Christian funerary meals, not only preparing the meals, but also leading them. Women raised a cup at funerary meals to toast the dead and led the group in liturgical recitations.[33] There were two places of meeting for early Christians: the "*house church*" (*domus ecclesiae*) and the cemetery. Also cross marks were found

---

[33] Ibid., 57.

on Christian ossuaries. However, the cross marks probably would have been protective taus rather than Christian crosses, which function to protect the burial from being disturbed by evil spirits. These cross marks are also found in Jewish funerary inscriptions, including those found in Roman catacombs. Thus, Christian burial rites are indistinguishable from Jewish ones in many respects. According to Byron McCane, Christian burials in Palestine cannot be clearly distinguished from Jewish burials until the late fourth century.[34] This means that standard Jewish burial practices continued among Jewish Christians for hundreds of years in Palestine.[35] Probably around the late fourth century, the Christian *"Cult of the dead"* and the cult of martyrs were growing in popularity, while rabbinic writers were encouraging increased distance from the dead and from cemeteries.

---

[34] Ibid., 58.
[35] Ibid., 59.

Christians gathered for meals, but for meals that featured bread and fish rather than bread and wine. Sometimes, but not always, wine was shared. The food was accompanied by cups and other utensils. It seems more likely that the fish depicted on tables with bread in Christian catacomb meal scenes was derived from the ancient use of fish in funerary offerings, and was eventually combined with Eucharistic motifs due to the celebration of the Eucharist as part of funerary meals. Christian women participated in these rituals, and also played roles as professional mourners.

In sum, women's tomb visitation and lamentation were prominent throughout the cultures of the ancient Mediterranean world. However, in addition to being stereotyped as overly emotional, women's tomb visitation and lamentation also came to have necromantic overtones more so than men's, even though men too are described as participating in funerals, magical practices, and conjuring of the dead at tombs. According to Corley, "*Necromancy is the invocation of spirits of the dead for the purposes of fortune-telling.*"[36] Ancient people believed that the tomb was the most likely place for an appearance of a departed spirit, the tomb being their "*house*," as it were. The spirits of those who had died an untimely or violent death such as murder or execution were considered especially powerful. Since lamentation was done by the gravesite, women associated dirges with the raising of the dead at tombs, and thereby with necromancy and magical arts. Those men who were involved in such ritual arts were called prophets, but the women were called witches. The best-known story from the Hebrew Bible involving necromancy is about a woman, the so-called Witch of Endor, who raises the spirit of the dead prophet Samuel for Saul. The spirit of Samuel then engages in a conversation with Saul (1 Sam. 28:3-19).

---

[36] Ibid., 40.

The woman's necromancy described in 1 Samuel must be a stereotypical religious ritual of women in the ancient Near East. Even later the Jewish writer Josephus had no trouble admitting that Samuel was raised by means of the woman's power.[37] Thus it is probable that many women participated not only in the funerary rituals, but also necromancy. As a result, women played significant roles in people's lives, especially since they were responsible for attending to the births and deaths of individuals. Many in the ancient world apparently found this dangerous, since Greek, Roman, and Jewish cultures tried to reduce women's roles in funerary rituals. It is evident in the Bible, since the other canonical gospel traditions such as Matthew, Luke, and John show more male involvement in the Easter narrative compared to the earliest written empty tomb narrative from the Gospel of Mark.

---

[37] Ibid., 49.

These funerary rituals present in various cultures were generally not practiced on behalf of those who died as criminals. Indeed, in Roman culture, funeral rites were often denied to criminals and traitors. Family members and close associates of the condemned could purchase the remains of the dead or even steal them. Corley states that

> "*The denial of burial and funeral rites was part of the punishment meted out to the condemned. Those executed for treason, particularly by means of crucifixion, were more likely to be denied basic burials and funeral rites. Some officials might show clemency by granting bodies to the family of the deceased, but this was probably exceptional. It should be remembered that there is some evidence that women as well as men, particularly slave women and women of the lower classes, could be arrested and even executed by means of impalement, crucifixion, or beheading.*"[38]

If indeed this was the case in Roman culture, Corley's research sheds light on the Gospels' passion narratives. It may bear particular significance for our

---

[38] Ibid., 31.

understanding of Mark's presentation of the silence of the

three women who visited the tomb of Jesus.

Historical and Literary Context of

Mark 16

In the Gospel of Mark, Jesus is portrayed as a political rebel. According to Brian Blount, *"The Jewish leaders charge Jesus with threatening not only their political power, but indeed the very socioeconomic structure on which the people depend. Jesus' attack on the temple-state is portrayed as a revolutionary call for social change that would leave everyone in socioeconomic and political disrepair."*[39] This means that Jesus' messianic work bears potent political implications. Jesus was crucified for political reasons, which may well have meant that burial and funerary rituals for him were disallowed.

---

[39] Brian K. Blount., *Cultural Interpretation: Reorienting New Testament Criticism* (Eugene, OR: Wipf and Stock Publishers, 1995), 156.

But according to the Markan narrative, Joseph of

Arimathea, who is identified as a prominent member of the

Jewish council, boldly asked Pilate for the body for Jesus

for burial – a request which Pilate grants (Mark 15:43-45).

The three women who visit the tomb in the following

verses were peasants, lower class members of the society.

If it were observed by others that they were visiting the

tomb of Jesus to perform funerary practices, their lives

could have been in danger. Indeed, if it were known that

they were going to Jesus' tomb to anoint his body, they

could perhaps have been arrested and even executed. Even

though the messenger at the tomb specifically commanded

them to tell the disciples and Peter of Jesus' resurrection,

the three women may have found it difficult to trust even

the disciples of Jesus. One of them, after all, had betrayed

him. Could this not shed some light on the fear and silence

with which Mark's Gospel concludes? I think this is an

interesting perspective to consider, given what we know of Roman funerary practices.

Women's funerary rituals in the ancient Mediterranean world show that they played a central role in preparing corpses for burial, preparing the funerary meals, and performing lamentations. The three women in the text, Mary Magdalene, Mary the mother of James, and Salome would have been very busy after the Sabbath, since at the very least they had to prepare funerary meals. However, in the empty tomb narrative that concludes the Gospel of Mark, they do not prepare the funerary meals, they do not cry or weep, and they do not beat their breasts or seek to place a coin in Jesus' mouth. They are described simply as coming to anoint the body of Jesus. Given that Jesus has already been anointed for burial in Mark 14 (14:3), could this be a sign that they, like the male disciples, are "*not getting it*"? In the Gospel of John, Joseph and Nicodemus place about seventy-five pounds of spices on Jesus (John 19:39), but according to the Gospel of Mark, Joseph of Arimathea did not anoint the body of Jesus. Joseph simply bought some linen cloth, took down the body, wrapped it in the linen, and placed it in a tomb cut out of rock (Mark 15:46). Since Mary Magdalene and Mary the mother of James saw this, maybe they wanted to provide a proper burial or funerary ritual for Jesus, even if it meant placing their lives in danger. However, as it turns out, they could not anoint the body of Jesus. He was not there. As the messenger conveyed to them, *"He has been raised"* (16:6). Although the women in the text go to the tomb of Jesus to perform tasks of corpse preparation expected of females in ancient cultures, the women in Mark do not conform to stereotyped gender expectations by mourning and lamenting. They followed Jesus, they remained with Jesus to the end, and they were commissioned to carry the news of resurrection to Jesus' male disciples.

In general, most scholars think the author of the
Gospel of Mark relied more heavily on oral tradition than
on materials that had previously been put into writing.[40]
While some sayings and stories employed by Mark no
doubt accurately preserve what the historical Jesus said and
did in the pre-Easter settings of Galilee and Jerusalem, their
value does not depend on their accuracy as history.[41] It is
possible that the evangelist Mark could have been familiar
with ascension accounts or stories of deification of certain
individuals. In Roman tradition, for example, there was a
story of Romulus, the founder of the city of Rome who
disappeared on the Nones of July, the month then called
Quintilis. A noble, Julius Proculus testified that Romulus
appeared to him as he was ascending to heaven, dressed in

---

[40] Mark Allan Powell, *Fortress Introduction to the Gospels*
(Minneapolis, MN: Fortress Press, 1998), 40.

[41] M. Eugene Boring, Fred B. Craddock., *The People's New Testament
Commentary* (Louisville, KY: Westminster John Knox Press, 2009),
105.

bright and shinning armor. The author of the Gospel of Mark was probably aware of the tradition that some Roman emperors had ascended to heaven.[42] Thus there may be a chance that the author of the Gospel of Mark incorporated this tradition with the empty tomb tradition to tell a story about God working through Jesus.

The oldest Jewish text that clearly expresses the idea of the resurrection of individual, physically dead people is the Book of the Watchers, which was later incorporated into a composite work known today as 1 Enoch.[43] The affirmation of followers of Jesus concerning him was that he had been raised from the dead as a single individual. This affirmation seemed quite similar to the claims that Enoch, Elijah, Romulus, and others had been taken, including their earthly bodies, to heaven. Since the earliest recoverable form of the Gospel of Mark does not

---

[42] Adela Yarbro Collins, *Mark: A Commentary*, Hermeneia (Minneapolis, MN: Fortress Press, 2007), 793.
[43] Collins, 783.

depict Jesus as walking the earth in bodily form, it is likely that the author assumed that his body had been taken from the tomb by God.[44] Also, I can see a progression of the idea of resurrection from the Gospel of Mark to Matthew and John, to Luke-Acts to Apocryphal Gospels. The earliest tradition about the resurrection linked it indissolubly with the exaltation of Jesus. Later, accounts of the resurrection appearances began to imply that, when Jesus rose from the dead, he returned to a bodily existence much like the one he had had before his death.

The author of the Gospel of Mark composed the empty tomb narrative on the basis of the tradition that on Easter Sunday morning women visited Jesus' tomb and found it empty and on the early Christian kerygma that Jesus was crucified, buried and raised on the third day. The three days consist of Friday before sunset, the Sabbath or Saturday, and Saturday evening and Sunday morning. The

---

[44] Ibid., 794.

third day is significant for the Old Testament; it is the decisive day for national restoration or resurrection. According to Hosea 6:2, *"After two days he will revive us; on the third day he will raise us up, that we may live for him."*[45] The narrative of Jesus' resurrection on the third day may convey that the empty tomb signifies the beginning of a new eschatological era, the beginning of the restoration of the people of God.

The empty tomb narrative with which the Gospel of Mark concludes can be viewed as an epilogue that provides the retrospective key to the whole Gospel. The epilogue is also the climax of the Gospel. The absence of a resurrection appearance puts the emphasis on the life Jesus lived. In this narrative, three women who were devoted to Jesus appeared to complete the burial process. There are many surprises in this narrative. The stone has been rolled

---

[45] John R. Donahue, Daniel J. Harrington., *The Gospel of Mark*, Sacra Pagina Series (Collegeville, MN: The Liturgical Press, 2002), 459.

away and Jesus has been raised. Those surprises are conveyed, grammatically, by the divine passive, indicating that it was God who rolled back the stone and raised Jesus from the dead. The language and grammar of the text clearly indicate that God is in control of the narrative.

Also, the narrative features the message of the angelic figure. The angelic figure announces the resurrection of Jesus, and commands the women to spread the message. So this is a Greek divine epiphany. In Greek literature, fear is a common reaction to a divine epiphany. The text features a dramatic vocabulary of fear. The women are described as "*alarmed*" to see the angelic figure, as fleeing the tomb in fear, and as saying nothing to anyone because of fear.

I resonate with what Mary Ann Beavis says about the community of Mark. She believes this text and the Gospel of Mark as a whole reflect a fearful community (e.g., 4:40, 6:51, 9:32, 10:32, 16:8).[46] However, this text is written with the expectation that the readers will be motivated by the narrative to pick up their crosses, to follow and to act.[47] In fact, one of the purposes of the Gospel of Mark is to reinforce in various ways the beliefs and identity of the readers as followers of Jesus.[48] The way that the Gospel ends can thus be understood in light of the impact it has on its readers.

The Gospel of Mark was written on the basis of living Christian tradition from and about Jesus that circulated in his church as the substance of preaching and teaching, including pre-Markan collections of materials.[49] Many scholars think that the empty tomb story was a

---

[46] Mary Ann Beavis., *Mark*, Paideai (Grand Rapids, MI: Baker Academic, 2011), 11.

[47] Beverly Roberts Gaventa, Patrick D. Miller., *The Ending of Mark and the Ends of God* (Louisville, KY: Westminster John Knox Press, 2005), 23.

[48] Kelly R. Iverson, Christopher W. Skinner., *Mark as Story: Retrospect and Prospect* (Atlanta, GA: Society of Biblical Literature, 2011), 118.

[49] M. Eugene Boring, *Mark*, The New Testament Library (Louisville, KY: Westminster John Knox Press, 2006), 13.

legend that developed around a cult associated with the
tomb in Jerusalem.[50] As I noted above, this argument could
have been a possibility. The detailed reference to the
women in 16:1 indicates that this unit of tradition existed at
one time independent from the passion narrative.[51] The
fact that women were the first to receive the announcement
of the resurrection is significant in view of attitudes then
current about women. According to Craig Evans, *"the
major factor that supports the historicity of the empty tomb
tradition is the potentially awkward admission that the
tomb was first visited by women, not Jesus' leading male
disciples,"*[52] even though Jewish law pronounced women
ineligible as witnesses. Additionally it would have been
shameful for the male disciples and male members of the

---

[50] Pheme Perkins., *The Gospel of Mark*, The New Interpreter's Bible vol. VIII (Nashville, TN: Abingdon Press, 1994), 730.
[51] William L. Lane., *The Gospel of Mark*, NICNT. (Grand Rapids, MI: William B. Eerdmans Publishing Company, 1974), 585.

[52] Craig A. Evans, *Mark 8:27-16:20*, Word Biblical Commentary (Nashville, TN: Thomas Nelson Publishers, 2001), 531.

community of the Gospel of Mark to hear that women

received the message of the resurrection first. Early

Christian tradition confirms that the reports of the women

concerning the empty tomb and Jesus' resurrection were

disregarded or considered embarrassing (Luke 24:11). That

the news had first been delivered by women was

inconvenient and troublesome to the Church, for their

testimony lacked value as evidence. The primitive

community would not have invented this detail, which can

be explained only on the ground that it was factual.[53]

---

[53] Ibid., 589.

Mark 16:1-8

Translation of the Text

> **TT**
>
> *When the Sabbath was over, Mary Magdalene, and Mary the mother of James, and Salome bought spices, so that they might go and anoint him. And very early in the morning on the first day of week, they came to the tomb, when the sun had risen. And they kept saying to one another, "Who will roll away the stone for us from the entrance of the tomb?"*
>
> *And when they looked up they saw that the stone had been rolled away – for the stone was extremely large. And as they entered into the tomb, they saw a young man sitting on the right side, dressed in a white robe, and they were distressed. But he said to them, "Don't be distressed. You are seeking Jesus the Nazarene, the Crucified One. He*

> *has been raised. He is not here. Look, the place where*
>
> *they laid him. But*[54] *go, tell his disciples, and even Peter*
>
> *that he is going ahead of you in*[55] *Galilee. Then you will*
>
> *see him there, just as he told you all.*
>
> *And they came out and fled from the tomb, for*
>
> *terror and ecstasy were holding them. And they said*
>
> *nothing to anyone. For they were afraid...*[56]

Outline

vv.1-4: The women's journey to the tomb.
vv.5-7: The women's encounter with a young man in the
    tomb.
vv.8: The women's flight from the tomb.

I read 16:1-8 as the original ending of the Gospel of

Mark. It is clear that 16:1 introduces a new scene. The

---

[54] The strong adversative conjunction is important. The women cannot remain at the tomb.

[55] εἰς means '*into.*' The term is used in place of "ἐν" frequently in the Gospel of Mark

[56] φοβέομαι is used throughout the Gospel of Mark to describe the failures of the disciples and the others.

previous unit is the narrative of the burial of Jesus by Joseph from Arimathea, and this text then presents an empty tomb narrative. So the beginning of the unit seems clear, but the ending of the text may seem uncertain. The sudden ending at v.8 has been explained in various ways. It is possible that the author died or was prevented from finishing his work. A second possibility is that the last page of the Gospel of Mark was lost. A third possibility is that the author intended to conclude at v.8.[57] Even though there is still ongoing debate about the ending of the Gospel of Mark, I would argue that the v.8 is the original and intended conclusion to the Gospel of Mark. Even though many of my fellow Korean Christians would have a hard time accepting this theory due to their theological conviction, I have to believe vv.9-20 represent a later addition to the Gospel, as do most modern scholars, on the basis of both internal and external text-critical evidence. In

---

[57] Donahue., 460.

Korean Christian ecclesial contexts, questioning the received biblical tradition is not common. Since many Korean editions of the Bible do not enclose vv.9-20 in brackets or identify it as a later addition, and since both Korean and Korean-American Christians are not accustomed, they have a tendency to read verses 9 through 20 as the originally intended ending of the Gospel of Mark. Even speaking of *"the original ending of the Gospel of Mark"* occasion discomfort for many Korean and Korean-American Christians, because it is not something that they grew up hearing from preachers and teachers. However, textual critics have demonstrated that vv. 9-20 do not exist in our earliest and best Greek manuscripts (e.g., Sinaiticus, Vaticanus, Sinaitic Syriac, about a hundred Armenian, and the two oldest Georgian manuscripts).

Some who find it hard to accept 16:8 as Mark's original and intended ending point to the unusual way in which v.8 ends, mid-sentence, with a dangling *gar* ("*for*").

However, scholars have demonstrated that ending with *gar*

would be unusual, but not impossible. Examples from

Greek literature of sentences that end with *gar* have been

noted. For example, in the Septuagint's version of Genesis

18:15, when Sarah encountered the angel of the Lord, the

narrative ends with a phrase, ἐφοβήθη γάρ.[58] Also, it was

standard literary practice in ancient writings to allude to

well-known events that occurred after those being narrated

in the text, without actually narrating those later events.

The best known example of this technique is in the Iliad.[59]

Ancient writing intended to do something to the

reader, to make people act or believe or change their

behavior, not just to entertain them with a suitably

---

[58] Joel Marcus, *Mark 8 – 16*, The Anchor Yale Bible (Binghamton, NY: Yale University Press, 2009), 1082.
[59] Collins., 797.

concluded literary experience.[60] So v.8 emphasizes the absence of Jesus in the time of the author and audiences, and the readers to be invited in the narrative. Additionally, the sudden break of a narrative at v.8, or the failure of the three women followers may prompt the intended audience to act faithfully to finish the story by following Jesus. Thus I do believe that chapter 16:1-8 is a unit with an appropriate concluding boundary.

Many Korean Christians believe that the Gospel of Mark was written by an individual named Mark. However, Mark's narrative provides no explicit information about the author's identity, location, or circumstances. The name "*Mark*" does not even appear in the Gospel. The titles of the Gospels are dated to the second century, when early Church fathers begin to refer to Gospels according to

---

[60] Carol A. Newsom, Sharon H. Ringe., *Women's Bible Commentary* (Louisville, KY: Westminster John Knox Press, 1998), 362.

Matthew, Mark, Luke, and John.[61] The name Mark was a
common name in the Roman Empire, and appears several
times throughout the NT, but never in the Gospels. Mark is
not listed as one of the twelve disciples of Jesus.
Traditionally, John Mark was referred to as the author and
the interpreter of Peter, according to the fourth century
historian Eusebius.[62] Thus according to Eusebius, the
location of the Gospel of Mark and church was *"in Babylon"*
(1 Pet. 5:13) – an early Christian code word for Rome.
Even today many contemporary scholars continue to argue
for the Roman provenance of the Gospel. However, the
Claudian expulsion of Jews from Rome in 49 C.E., the
author's use and occasional explanations of Aramaic terms
to his audience (5:41; 7:34; 9:5; 11:21; 14:36; 15:34), and
special geographical attention to Galilee suggest to me that

---

[61] Beavis, 6.
[62] Beavis, 7.

the Gospel of Mark was written either in Galilee or nearby

southern Syria.

On the Way to the Tomb

In this text, the term μνημεῖον ("*tomb*") appears four

times: twice as the women go to the tomb, once when the

women were in the tomb, and once as the women flee from

the tomb. So this text can be divided into three

subdivisions on the basis of this movement and repetition:

the women's journey to the tomb, into the tomb, and out of

the tomb.

The three faithful women, Mary Magdalene, Mary

the mother of James and Salome have witnessed the

crucifixion from afar (15:40), and two Marys witnessed

Joseph's burial of Jesus (15:47). "*Mary the mother of*

James" in our Greek text is "*Μαρία ἡ [τοῦ] Ἰακώβου.*"

The woman is the same one mentioned in 15:40, which

notes the presence of "*Mary, the mother of James the*

younger and Joses." Her identification is abbreviated[63] in this text. The Gospel of Mark introduced a woman named Mary who has sons named James and Joses in 6:3, who may be Jesus' own mother[64] even though the Gospel of Mark never explicitly identifies her as such. The names "*Mary Magdalene, and Mary the mother of James, and Salome*" (16:1), and the forms in which they appear, may display cultural norms. Historically, women were not identified by their own names, but by their relationship to men, whether father, husband, son, or son-in-law.[65] Yet the narrative of the Gospel of Mark seems to break with the traditional patriarchal, androcentric pattern at significant points. Mary Magdalene appears in the story without any association with a male head of household. The phrase "*Μαρία ἡ Μαγδαληνὴ*" can be translated as Mary from

---

[63] Collins, 794.

[64] Janice Capel Anderson, Stephen D. Moore., *Mark and Method* (Minneapolis, MN: Fortress Press, 2008), 86.

[65] Richard A. Horsley, *Hearing the Whole Story* (Louisville, KY: Westminster John Knox Press, 2001), 204.

Magdala, simply identifying her with her hometown. The second Mary is identified by her sons, and the last character, Salome is identified only by name. The advent of Roman imperial rule in Palestine brought acute pressure on the viability of the patriarchal family and a breakdown in patriarchal authority. In their conquest and reconquest, the Roman armies would have killed or enslaved a disproportionate number of young men. Also, Herod Antipas' building of two capital cities within twenty years in the tiny area of Lower Galilee, which required massive numbers of laborers, probably disrupted traditional patterns of family and village life. Additionally, the historian Josephus indicates that many thousands of workers labored in the reconstruction of the Temple in Jerusalem for nearly eighty years.[66] These names, "*Mary Magdalene, and Mary the mother of James, and Salome,*" may well reflect the deteriorating conditions of family and village life at the

---

[66] Horsley, 220.

time. It may also provide another explanation for the absence of male presence as three women take the journey to the tomb.

Nevertheless, after the twelve chosen disciples fled, betrayed, or denied Jesus, he died alone on the cross, and was buried by a non-disciple of Jesus. The women characters exemplify the way of discipleship amid the failure and absence of the male disciples. Their fear and failure are juxtaposed with the courage and faithfulness of the women, whose actions frame and hold together the final act of the Gospel of Mark.[67] In a Korean cultural context, the male disciples of Jesus would not only be seen as failing to embrace the discipleship that Jesus was teaching them, but also as failing to embody " 정" (Jeong). In Korean contexts "*Jeong*" saturates daily living and all forms of relationships. As a cultural concept and practice,

---

[67] Ibid., 72.

"*Jeong*" encompasses but is not limited to notions of compassion, affection, solidarity, vulnerability, and forgiveness. According to Wonhee Anne Joh, "*Many Koreans often feel that Jeong is more powerful, lasting, and transformative than love. Jeong makes relationships "sticky" but also recognizes the complex and dynamic nature of all relationalism.*"[68] "*Jeong*" may seem to be a form of love. Yet "*Jeong*" is difficult to categorize in relation to the notions of love that have often been fragmented as *eros, philia, and agape*. As Wonhee Anne Joh says, "*Jeong*" is "*sticky*," and I would say it has a strong sense of relationality. Jeong is an intentional, wise, and knowing decision to relinquish that recognizes not only one's own dignity and worth, but also that of others. To suggest that someone does not have "*Jeong*" would be a harsh insult in Korean and Korean American culture. Since

---

[68] Rita Nakashima Brock, Jung Ha Kim, Kwow Pui-Lan, Seug Ai Yang., *Off the Menu: Asian and Asian North American Women's Religion and Theology* (Louisville, KY: Westminster John Knox Press, 2007), 147.

the male disciples of Jesus did not stay with him when he
was arrested, were not present at his crucifixion, and did
not even visit his tomb, many Koreans would see the male
disciples not only as failing Jesus, but also as not
embodying "*Jeong.*"

The Gospel of Mark never explicitly indentifies the
three women who visit Jesus' tomb as "*disciples.*"
However, their behaviors are described with Markan
language that implies discipleship, e.g., the language of
ἀκολουθέω ("*following*") in chapter 15:41.[69] This language
also conveys their courage and commitment to Jesus, in
contrast to his male disciples. I do not think it can be said
Mark depicts them as "*non-disciples*" in contrast to the
disciples of Jesus. When Jesus called his male disciples,
the Twelve in chapter 3, he invited them to "ἵνα ὦσιν μετ'
αὐτοῦ"(3:14) which means, "*so that they may be with me.*"

---

[69] Brian K. Blount, *Go Preach!: Mark's Kingdom Message and the
Black Church Today* (Maryknoll, NY: Orbis Books, 1998), 188.

Jesus called his disciples not only to proclaim the gospel of God and join him in ministry, but also to accompany him. However, when the male disciples sensed imminent danger, they failed to stick with him. Nevertheless, the text tells us that the three women bought spices and went to the tomb to anoint Jesus. They probably thought that Jesus' burial has been left incomplete. The reader is likely to find this a hopeful sign, and to be relieved that some of Jesus' followers remained true to him.[70]

Several years ago, I taught this text to the Korean-American congregation that I have been ministering to for the last four and a half years. After I read the text, one Korean American high school student observed out loud that the women were not "religious, pious, or faithful," because they did not say anything to anyone. I pointed out to him that the women were religious enough to keep the Sabbath. The Greek text suggests that they set out on their

---

[70] Newsom, 361.

journey to the tomb διαγενομένου τοῦ σαββάτου which

means *"when the Sabbath was over,"* which is a genitive

absolute. The phrase indicates that it was about after 6:00

P.M. Saturday, the time when the women would have been

permitted to purchase items and to engage in work, such as

preparing perfumes and ointments for Jesus' body.[71] They

were faithful enough to buy ἀρώματα which means spices

or perfume, with which to anoint Jesus' body. Spices were

used to prepare bodies for burial, or to remove bad smells.

This was a service not only to the dead, but also to the

survivors who would have to spend time with the corpse in

the burial chamber as part of the funeral ceremony.[72] After

the women finished the preparation for the visitation, they

began their journey very early in the morning. The phrase,

"καὶ λίαν πρωΐ ... ἀνατείλαντος τοῦ ἡλίου" means *"very*

early in the morning ... when the sun had risen," or *"after*

---

[71] Evans, 534.
[72] Marcus, 1079.

the sun had risen, very early in the morning." The construction is a typically Markan two-step progression, in which the second phrase qualifies the first.[73] The genitive absolute in the second phrase is in an emphatic position.[74] This detail may underline their dedication and faithfulness to Jesus. The three women were not wasting any time. According to Mark's passion narrative, Jesus died on the cross at *"the ninth hour"* (15:34-37) which is about three o'clock in the afternoon. So for about twenty-seven hours the women could do nothing after watching Joseph of Arimathea bury Jesus (15:45-47), except perhaps to weep and commemorate him. But they started getting ready to properly anoint the body of Jesus the moment they were allowed, and departed as soon as they were able.

As the women were on their journey to the tomb, they questioned one another. The imperfect verb, ἔλεγον

---

[73] Collins, 795.
[74] Marcus, 1083.

indicates that they did so repeatedly. They kept asking,

"Who will roll the stone away from the entrance of the

tomb for us?" (16:3). This question sounds a bit odd, as it

appears they gave no forethought to the matter of who

would provide access to the tomb. If the mother of James

was the mother of Jesus, she could have grabbed her sons

for assistance in anointing their brother. In other respects

they planned ahead for the visit, purchasing spices or

perfume, so it is unlikely to think that they failed to

consider the stone at the entrance of the tomb.   The stone

used to seal the openings to tombs were anywhere from

five to six feet in diameter with varying thickness.[75]

Donahue and Harrington state that the use of a *"large flat*

circular stone that could be rolled into a groove cut out of

the rock" to prevent tomb-robbing was typical of this kind

of burial.[76] They witnessed Joseph's burial of Jesus, so

---

[75] Evans, 535.
[76] Donahue and Harrington. 455.

they saw how big the stone was. Also, they most likely remembered that the stone blocked the entrance of the tomb. Thus it is unlikely that they had not thought about asking someone to help them. Maybe they did not have anyone who was willing to help them, in which case the question might underline the absence of Jesus' male disciples. If I read this verse as a question, the women do not seem to be very plan oriented, but this would be uncharacteristic of these women in the Gospel of Mark so far. They planned the visitation of the tomb, they planned to buy spices, they were courageous and even economically able to follow Jesus and care for his needs (15:41). Thus in my view, the women's question may be a lament rather than a real question.[77] This lament emphasizes both that the women have no expectation of finding the stone rolled away,[78] and it may also highlight the absence of Jesus' disciples.

---

[77] Marcus, 1079.
[78] Boring, 444.

Additionally, the ancient funerary rituals entrusted to

women suggest that lament was a prominent practice done

by women. Thus it can be read as a lament, one that helps

readers prepare for the surprise.[79]

A great surprise is waiting for the women at the

entrance of the tomb. When they reach it, they saw that the

large stone had been rolled away, although it was really

large. The verb θεωροῦσιν means *"they see, observe,*

perceive, or experience." But since it is a historical present,

I translated as *"they saw."* The verb is used in the Gospel

of Mark for beholding spectacles and significant events,

and it is used in each of the three scenes where the three

women appear:[80] the crucifixion of Jesus, the burial of

Jesus, and the empty tomb narrative. The women just do

not θεωροῦσιν, but ἀναβλέψασαι θεωροῦσιν. The verb

ἀναβλέπω conveys not just physical sight, but rather

---

[79] Donahue and Harrington, 458.
[80] R. Alan Culpepper, *Mark*, Smyth & Helwys Bible Commentary
(Macon, GA: Smyth & Helwys Publishing, 2007), 585.

something more. The verb βλέπω is used for correct

spiritual discernment that would protect the disciple from

being misled by external appearances (10:51). Thus when

they saw or looked up, something spectacular happened.

The stone had been rolled away. The verb form of

ἀποκεκύλισται is a perfect passive. It is a divine passive, an

example of the passive voice being used to avoid speaking

directly of God.[81] The readers are to understand that the

rolling back of the stone was an act of God. This past act

of God is conveyed by the perfect tense, indicating that it

definitely affects the present. The stone has been rolled

away once and for all time.[82]

The stone that blocked the journey of the three

women to Jesus seemed extremely large in human

perspective, and human understanding. Blockages or

boundaries may exist in our faith journey to Jesus. We may

---

[81] Lamar Williamson Jr., *Mark*, Interpretation (Louisville, KY: John
Knox Press, 1983), 284.
[82] Boring, 444.

feel helpless and lament obstacles before us that seem impossible to move. However, our God understands that. He is capable of moving it, and He is willing to move it. If the three women had some assistance from other characters to move the stone, the narrative would not have underlined as emphatically the action of God. On the other hand, since the women were without assistance, it was clearly God who intervened in their journey to the tomb, and rolled away the stone.

In the Tomb

In sum, by means of the divine passive, readers know exactly who rolled away the stone, but the three faithful women do not. It could have been a trap, or someone could have opened the tomb to steal the body of Jesus and so forth. It was not a normal and expected situation that the women faced. It could have been a dangerous situation, especially for a group of three women early in the morning, but they do not hesitate to go inside the tomb. Maybe their spiritual discernment, spiritual perception (16:4) gave them courage to proceed. Thus far, the narrative holds out hope that at least these three women will embody faithfulness to Jesus.

As the women entered into the tomb, they faced more surprises. They saw a young man sitting on the right

side dressed in a white robe. The only other time the word
νεανίσκος is used in the Gospel of Mark is in 14:51 in the
description of the young man who ran away naked in the
arrest scene. But if the young man here were identical with
the young man of ch.14, he would be introduced as ὁ
νεανίσκος and not simply as νεανίσκος. Mary Ann Beavis
notes a striking possibility for the identity of the young man.
She observes that the young man could have been the risen
Jesus, *"existing in an angelified state, like Enoch, Elijah,*
and Moses, transfigured and clothed in garments of shining
white."[83]

Koreans see this young man in the text as an angel,
a ghost, " 귀신" (Gui-Shin), simply a spiritual being. In
Korean common folk tales, spiritual beings appear and tell
human beings about the future, news, or commands.
Interestingly, the gender of spiritual beings is often

---

[83] Beavis. 244.

identified. For example, Sejong Chun tells a story about

Muno's sister who died and her spirit possessed her

brother's body, and caused problems in her village.[84]

There are male spiritual beings and female spiritual beings

in traditional Korean folk tales and their cultural

perspectives and understandings of spiritual beings.

According to Chun, "*It is commonly believed that in a*

patriarchal Confucian society such as the Chosun dynasty,

being born a woman meant han."[85] He defines "*han(한)* "

as "*A deeply repressed and accumulated emotion of sorrow,*

resentment, and helplessness."[86] Since being a female

meant "*han*" in traditional Korean society, generally when

female spiritual beings appear in folk tales, they are the

deceased sisters, mothers, or widows with "*han,*" and thus

do negative things to the living to express or release their

"*han.*" However, when male spiritual beings appear in the

---

[84] Duran. 21.
[85] Ibid, 22.
[86] Ibid., 29.

narratives, normally they are deceased male ancestors, or male kin members, generally leaders of a family to protect, guide, warn or bless their beloved living ones. Thus good things are expected in the narrative when male spiritual beings appear.

Given this cultural perspective, Korean readers may well be inclined to see the young man as Jesus. Jesus was a male, he formed his own "*family*," and he functioned as a leader of a family. The young man thus would appear in the narrative not to harm the women, but rather to convey positive news, command and comfort. Thus as a Korean American, I am able to consider the possibility that the young man could be the risen Jesus. But it is also likely that the character in the narrative is best defined as an angel. The motif of white or shining clothes typically characterizes angels and other heavenly beings[87] in the

Bible.

In the Old Testament and the Jewish literature from

the later period, angels frequently appear as divine

messengers of God. In the New Testament the color white

is primarily the heavenly color and is mentioned almost

exclusively in eschatological or apocalyptic contexts.[88] In

the Old Testament, ancient Jewish sources, and the New

Testament, angels have the appearance of human beings.

In the Book of Judges, an angel is called *"a man of God,"*

and in the Book of Acts, angels are referred to as *"two men*

in white robes" (Acts 1:10), and in the book of 2nd

Maccabees, the angel was called a *"young man"* (2 Mac.

3:26). Mark's text bears similarities to such angelophanies,

which usually include an introductory identification of

those to whom an angel appears, a description of the

---

[87] Collins, 795.

[88] Lane, 587.

angel's appearance, a reference to the recipients' fear, a word of consolation from the angel, a word of revelation, and usually a word of command.[89] Thus this youth is probably to be understood as an angel, the divine messenger of God, even though the Gospel of Mark never explicitly identifies him as such.

Even though I do see this young man as an angelic figure, it could be read in a different way. The only other time the word, νεανίσκος is used in the Gospel of Mark is in 14:51 in the description of the young man who ran away naked at Jesus' arrest. The text notes that "*they got hold of him*," so I have a sense that the people were trying to grab the young man but as he tried to run away, he found himself naked. This would suggest an involuntary stripping of clothing. The involuntary stripping of clothing by another is humiliating and shaming.[90] Even the ancients

---

[89] Marcus, 1080.
[90] Neyrey, 25.

agreed that clothes made the man, for they signaled honorable role and status, while their absence implied shame. Thus the young man in the scene of Jesus' arrest was a shamed character. However, in the text of the empty tomb, the young man is sitting on the right side, the generally honored position,[91] and wearing a *"white"* robe. A *"white"* robe or white clothing was worn by singers in Solomon's temple (2 Chron. 5:12), and angelic messengers were generally clad in *"white"* garments. In the Book of Revelation, the elders seated around the throne of God (Rev. 4:4), the martyrs (Rev. 6:11), as well as the heavenly army are all clothed in white (Rev. 19:14).[92] Similarly, white garments are pure, not soiled, thus reflecting righteousness, and even Jesus' clothes were white and shinning in the scene of the Transfiguration. Thus, *"white"* suggest heavenly things or beings, but also honorable ones. The

---

[91] Ibid., 24.
[92] Ibid., 63.

physical person or one's body is normally a symbolic

representation of the social value of honor. Honor and

shame are displayed when the body is crowned, anointed,

touched, covered, uncovered, held, cut off, struck, or

slapped.[93] The young man who fled in shame could thus be

viewed as one now restored in honor and proclaiming the

good news. This young man may have been the symbolic

representation of the community of Mark. When Jesus first

predicted his passion in Mark 8:31, he said, *"Those who are*

ashamed of me and of my words in this adulterous and

sinful generation, of them the Son of Man will also be

ashamed when he comes in the glory of his Father with the

holy angels." Greek words for honor, esteem, recognition

($\tau\iota\mu\dot{\eta}$), are commonly used of humans. They can also be

used in praise of God and Jesus with other terms like

δόξα.[94] During Jesus' first passion prediction, the term

---

[93] Malina, 39.
[94] Rohrbaugh, 23.

ἐπαισχύνομαι appears twice. Being honored or shamed by Jesus depends on one's valuing of Jesus and his words. The community of Mark perhaps fled for its own survival, perhaps during the Nero's persecutions of Christians in 64 C.E., or during the Jewish War in 66-73 C.E.. Perhaps they simply laid low. But that community, which did not want to be shamed by Jesus at the end of eschaton, could now be portrayed as claiming the resurrection, or the empty tomb narrative through its written document, the Gospel of Mark. Thus, I could also see the young man as a symbolic representation of the community of Mark.

When the women saw him, they were ἐξεθαμβήθησαν, which means *"they were alarmed."* It can also mean *"amazed"* or *"distressed."*[95] The compound verb is intensive, usually expressing great emotion.[96] The verb appears twice in the text, in verses 5 and 6, once by the

---

[95] Ibid, 587.
[96] Evans, 536.

narrator describing the emotion of the three women, the other by the angel to comfort the women. The women's response to an encounter with the angelic figure is a typical reaction ascribed to human beings in accounts of epiphanies of heavenly beings.[97] In such cases, the heavenly being often strengthens, comforts or reassures the recipient of the epiphany, as the young man does in v. 6. The only other time the term ἐκθαμβέω was used in the Gospel of Mark was in the narrative of Gethsemane to describe the emotion of Jesus in 14:33. I do not think that Jesus was amazed at the event that was about to come to him, but was more likely anxious or distressed. Since the same term is used only in ch.14 and this text, I would translate the emotion that the three women where feeling as "*distressed.*"

This angelic figure knows why the women have come, and identifies Jesus not in terms of christological

---

[97] Collins, 796.

titles, but only as the one from Nazareth, and as the

Crucified One. Jesus had been designated as τὸν

Ναζαρηνὸν three times previously in the Gospel of Mark:

by the unclean spirit in the synagogue at Capernaum (1:24),

by blind Bartimaeus (10:47), and by the high priest's maid

when questioning Peter (14:67).[98] So Jesus has never been

referred to in this way by his disciples. Whenever Jesus is

identified as the Nazarene, another descriptor accompanies

it in the narrative. The unclean spirit identified Jesus as the

Holy One of God after calling him the Nazarene in 1:24.

Bartimaeus called Jesus the Son of David after hearing that

Jesus the Nazarene was near in 10:47. In the narrative of

Peter's denial, when the high priest's maid referred to Jesus

as the Nazarene, Peter and Jesus are then referred to as

Galileans. It appears that every time Jesus is referred to as

the Nazarene, his ministerial titles follow. He is the Holy

One of God who preaches the gospel of God, he is the Son

---

[98] Donahue, 458.

of David who functions as the expected Messiah, and a

Galilean, since his primary public ministry was conducted

in Galilee. Those all seem to be correct, and important

titles of Jesus, but his own disciples never identify him as

the Nazarene, perhaps because they failed to see him as

such. In this text, a similar pattern follows. After the

angelic figure identifies Jesus as the Nazarene, he

accompanies it with another title. Jesus is τὸν

ἐσταυρωμένον, which means *"the one who has been*

crucified" or *"the Crucified One."* The perfect passive

participle indicates a past event whose reality continues

into the present. The crucifixion is not an episode in the

past that is left behind at the resurrection. Even as the risen

one, Jesus continues to be the one who has been crucified.[99]

This is another ministerial title of Jesus, and maybe the

early Christian church's confession. The use of this final

---

[99] Boring, 441.

title in reference to Jesus indicates that Jesus' identity and
ministry cannot be described apart from the cross. The
angelic figure gives another chance for the disciples and the
faithful women to realize that this is the proper confession
to recognize that this is at the heart of Jesus' identity.[100]

Then the angelic figure tells the women the message
that Jesus has been raised, using another divine passive
(ἠγέρθη). The passive verb is emphatic. Jesus does not
raise himself by his own power. He is raised by God's
power from the dead. Readers are to remember that it was
God who rolled the stone of the entrance of the tomb away,
and that same God raised Jesus from the dead. Thus the
empty tomb narrative has a decidedly theocentric focus.
The arrival of the reign of God was at the heart of Jesus'
preaching and ministry, and the message of the empty tomb
narrative has a similarly theocentric focus. By this

---

[100] Ched Myers, *Binding the Strong Man: A Political Reading of
Mark's Story of Jesus* (Maryknoll, NY: Orbis Books, 1988), 398.

narrative, the readers know that everything Jesus lived and died for points to God who was willing to rip the heavens apart to identify Jesus as Son and anoint him for ministry (1:10-11), who was willing to bring the Gentiles into the faith community (7:24-30), who ripped the Temple curtain from top to bottom at the moment of Jesus' death (15:38), and who raised Jesus from the dead. The Jewish authorities had arrested Jesus, the Roman authorities may have crucified him, and an extremely large stone blocked the door of his tomb, but even death, the ultimate enemy of human beings, could not bind Jesus, for God has the final say. Thus God raises Jesus. Then the angelic figure says, "*Look, the place where they laid him,*" which serves to emphasize the emptiness of the tomb.[101] It is not like the three women visited the wrong tomb, nor was only the spirit of Jesus raised. The dead body of Jesus is not at the

---

[101] Perkins, 730.

place where Joseph of Arimathea laid it. Jesus has really been raised, and by the power of God.

In Jesus' day, people in the ancient Mediterranean world viewed death as a reality that ended the possibility of achieving further success, and that could even signal defeat by a rival's superior power. Death by crucifixion climaxed a process of bodily degradation. It was preceded by torture and mutilation, and was occasionally accompanied by the condemned being forced to witness the brutal deaths of their wives and children. Moreover, victims whose children were executed could not count on their heirs to carry on their name or seek vengeance, both marks of shame. Crucifixion was indeed "*most cruel and disgusting, most evil, shameful, insulting*" punishment.[102] These descriptions indicate the common cultural perception that death by crucifixion constituted the worst imaginable fate, indeed, the most shameful of deaths. Also, Jesus is himself

---

[102] Neyrey, 140.

shamed by the thieves with whom he is crucified in 15:32, as they join the crowd in taunting him. Christians writing about the crucifixion of Jesus were confronted with a devastating event of genuine shame and stigma. The leader figure of the movement was executed in a manner suggestive of sedition: crucifixion was commonly associated with the punishment of political revolutionaries in the Roman Empire. Greeks and Romans might view Jesus, then, as a rebel who sought to overturn the peace.[103] If crucifixion meant radical shame because of loss of power, strength, life, honor, and beauty, rendering Jesus utterly shamed and disgraced, then God's resurrection of Jesus undoes that shame and restores his honor. Indeed, the highest of honors is ascribed to Jesus through resurrection.

Having assured the women that Jesus was raised, the angelic figure then says ὑπάγετε εἴπατε, which means, *"go tell."* The indicative of the resurrection message

---

[103] deSilva, 45.

contains a built-in imperative.[104] There is no reason for the women to stay at the tomb, for there is no dead body to anoint. The three women cannot stay in the tomb. They are commanded to depart from the empty tomb, and are also told to carry this message of Jesus' resurrection to the disciples καὶ τῷ Πέτρῳ. The Phrase *"and Peter"* could also be translated as *"especially Peter"* or *"even Peter."*[105] I would translate it as *"even Peter,"* who may need a special word of assurance given his denial of Jesus. Even though Peter shamefully denied Jesus, though he had promised Jesus that he would not, there still is the promise of healing and restoration.

---

[104] Boring and Craddock, 172.
[105] Ibid., 442.

Flight from the Tomb

God raised Jesus back from the dead, and the angelic figure tells the women to inform the disciples and even Peter, that Jesus is going ahead of them to Galilee. But the women fled from the tomb in fear, "*And they said nothing to anyone. For they were afraid*" (16:8). I generally agree with those who would argue that the common motif of fear during angelophanies in ancient and biblical writings illumines the women's fear. The woman may also be fearful since they have to go back to Galilee and start all over again, in service of the ministry of the Kingdom of God which got Jesus killed. But for this project, I want to read the last verse a little bit differently, through the lens of honor and shame. Honor came largely by living up to the values and social expectations into which individuals were socialized. Families or groups in the first-century world were not entirely self-sufficient and independent economically. Social life requires some degree of interdependence, cooperation, and shared enterprise. In the United States, an auto dealer will not sell you a new car unless your credit rating is good. In the ancient Mediterranean world, no one would freely associate with you in covenant relationship unless your honor rating was good, so a good name and family reputation were the most valuable of assets.[106] The family, tribe, village, city or ethnic group had its own norms and commonly shared meaning – a common sense, and a collective sense of identity. A person with common sense was respectable, reputable, and honorable. Thus the honorable person would never expose his or her distinct individuality. One's unique personhood, one's inner self – with its difficulties, weaknesses, confusions, and inabilities to cope, as well as

---

[106] Malina, 37.

its distinctive, individual real hopes and dreams – was

simply not of public concern or comment.[107] A woman

was not seen as an independent entity or agent but as

embedded in the identity and honor of some male (her

father or husband). A woman's words were for her

husband's ears, not for the public ear. The focus of ancient

people on honor and shame meant that they were

particularly oriented toward the approval and disapproval

of others. As a group discovered and defined those

qualities that it needed its members to display in order for

the group to survive, the desire to be honored would ensure

that the members would all do their part to promote the

health and survival of the group. Those who violated those

values were held in contempt.[108] Thus honoring and

shaming became the dominant means of enforcing all those

values that were not actually legislated and of reinforcing

---

[107] Malina, 59.
[108] deSilva, 36.

those values that were covered by written laws. The testimony of the three women would not have been valued or viewed as legitimate according to their cultural norms. If they went out and said something to someone, they would probably have been viewed as confused, dreaming or hoping, unable to cope with stress, and shameful. Also, maybe they feared being laughed at by their own community members, who would not have believed their testimony. Thus they were faced with a dilemma: they could either spread the good news, or behave according to social expectations placed upon them. That may be why *"they did not say anything to anyone."*

The flow of the narrative in the first half of the Gospel of Mark is from Galilee to Jerusalem. The second half of the Gospel's narrative traces Jesus' journey to the cross and the scattering of his disciples. Mark's ending shifts the focus back to Galilee and envisions a regathering

of the disciples. So now Mark reconstructs this
reconciliation of the disciples with Jesus in two stages: tell
the disciples, and Peter.[109] Throughout the Gospel of Mark,
the disciples of Jesus kept failing him, or misunderstanding
him. Other minor characters such as Bartimaeus, a woman
from Bethany who anointed Jesus, or these three faithful
women who followed Jesus from Galilee look like more
suitable disciples. However, that is precisely the point.
Jesus took unlikely candidates as his disciples, taught them,
showed them, and lived with them through his ministry in
service of the Kingdom of God. The disciples know what
the ministry of Jesus led to: crucifixion. But after he has
been raised, the angelic figure's message redirects the
disciples back to Galilee to continue the movement that
Jesus started there.[110]

---

[109] Myers, 398.
[110] Horsley, 48.

The anticipated meeting in Galilee promised restoration and forgiveness even for those who had abandoned and denied Jesus. Interestingly, Judas Iscariot, the betrayer of Jesus does not commit suicide or lose his life in the Gospel of Mark as in Matthew and Acts. Judas Iscariot was the betrayer, but still a disciple of Jesus. The angelic figure's command calls the disciples and even Peter to go to Galilee. Peter is singled out, which leads me to imagine that in the Gospel of Mark, at least, that the possibility of restoration is open to all disciples. Nevertheless, the narrative puts a spotlight on Peter. Jesus addressed Peter as Simon at Gethsemane, which was the last time Jesus spoke his name. Simon was Peter's name before Jesus called him as a disciple and renamed him. Thus it is striking that at Gethsemane Jesus reverts to the pre-discipleship name. But in the empty tomb narrative, Simon is again called "*Peter*," his discipleship name.[111]

---

[111] David Rhoads, Joanna Dewey, Donald Michi., *Mark as Story* 2nd ed.

The restoration was already beginning to take place in the empty tomb when the angelic messenger spoke of the promised meeting in Galilee. This is a very comforting point. The general thinking about the disciples in the Gospel of Mark is that they never measure up to Jesus' expectations. But Jesus never lets go of the disciples, and neither does the Gospel of Mark. Despite their failures it is clear that the author of the Gospel believes that Jesus has not finished with them yet.[112] Thus the Gospel of Mark is a story of discipleship. The angelic figure commissioned the three women to tell Jesus' disciples that they would be reunited with him in Galilee.[113] Galilee was the place of Jesus' announcement of the Kingdom of God, the place where the disciples had witnessed his teaching, the sea crossings, the exorcisms, and the meals with Jews and

---

(Minneapolis, MN: Fortress Press, 1999), 95.

[112] Brian K. Blount, *Then the Whisper Put on Flesh: New Testament Ethics in an African American Context* (Nashville, TN: Abingdon Press, 2001), 58.

[113] Lane, 589.

Gentiles.[114] This concluding focus on Galilee also suggests that God is no longer bound up with Jerusalem and its temple, and Jesus' message will reach Gentiles.[115]

The three women fled from the tomb in fear. The word ἔκστασις can mean *"astonishment"* in a positive sense, but it also can mean *"terror, or fear"* in a negative sense. The only other occurrence of the term in the Gospel of Mark is in 5:42, when Jesus raised Jairus' daughter from the dead. When Jesus told people at the house of Jairus that the daughter was not dead but sleeping, they laughed at him. However, when Jesus raised the girl from the dead, people felt ἔκστασις. According to Eugene Boring, *"At least in the Gospel of Mark, the word does not mean reverent amazement, but fear resulting in disobedience,"*[116] and disbelief. I would argue, however, that positive implications of this word may be present as well. Given

---

[114] Culpepper, 588.
[115] Boring, 447.
[116] Ibid., 442.

that the only two appearances of this word are in the

context of resurrection accounts, I can see people being

excited as well being terrified. The use of this verb in this

text may indicate that the women were ecstatic. They were

completely dominated by an intense emotion, probably an

intense emotion, that may well have entailed a measure of

excitement as well as great fear, and were not about to

follow the commands that the angelic figure gave them.

Also just as they did not hesitate to enter the tomb earlier in

v. 5, in v. 8 they do not hesitate to flee from the tomb, as if

they had nothing to do with the epiphany or the message

that they received from the angelic figure. When the three

faithful women encountered a young man in the tomb, they

were "*distressed*." After they heard the good news from

the angelic figure, they fled from the tomb in terror and

ecstasy, and said nothing to anyone. The phrase καὶ οὐδενὶ

οὐδὲν εἶπον, literally means, "*and they said nothing to no one.*" The double negative adds emphasis.[117] They said nothing to anyone because they were afraid. The imperfect tense of the verb ἐφοβοῦντο suggests that their fear was ongoing. The intense feelings that the women felt escalated as the empty tomb narrative unfolds. They felt distressed when they encountered the angelic figure, they felt terror and ecstasy after hearing the good news, and finally they felt fear. Those women were courageous enough to remain present during Jesus' crucifixion and burial, and to journey to his tomb. However, finally as they were experiencing the empty tomb, terror, ecstasy, and fear finally got hold of them, stopped them, and muted them.

---

[117] Evans., 538.

Conclusion

What were they afraid of? I do not think that the encounter with the angelic figure was the only reason for their fear. It had to be occasioned by more than just an angelophany. Were they afraid, perhaps, of the good news of the resurrection of Jesus? A living Lord would have been good news for them, since they were sincere and faithful to him. Perhaps they were afraid because Jesus' preaching of the Kingdom of God and embodiment of it in his boundary-breaking life and ministry resulted in crucifixion. By reuniting with him in Galilee, would his followers share a similar fate? I find this a more suitable explanation. However, the three faithful women do not spread the message.

Therefore, like the male disciples, the three women failed in their commission. The theme of human failure in the Gospel of Mark is complete. The religious authorities, Jesus' hometown, the disciples, the crowds, the Roman authorities, and even the three faithful women who had followed Jesus since his days in Galilee all failed Jesus. When the three women who had been faithful to this point finally failed as well, the readers' hopes are dashed. There is no one left to tell the story. No one, Tolbert notes, *"But the audience itself."*[118] The plot therefore draws the reader in as a participant. The narrator permitted only the readers to be *"with Jesus"* the whole time, and only the readers are left to act faithfully. The readers are to be the faithful followers or disciples of Jesus. To be a disciple is to accept the cross of Jesus as one's own. It is to accept suffering on

---

[118] Mary Ann Tolbert, *Sowing the Gospel: Mark's World in Literary – Historical Perspective* (Minneapolis, MN: Fortress Press, 1989), 297.

his behalf.[119] Discipleship is not exemplified by suffering; suffering is the tragic outcome of following Jesus. The community of Jesus' followers is called to live out their vocation of suffering discipleship without the immediate presence of Jesus.[120]

As I noted it above, ancient writings tended to encourage the readers to act. In this case of the original ending of the Gospel of Mark, the text is calling the readers to go preach and follow Jesus, even at the cost of losing their lives. That is a fear worthy message. But the Gospel of Mark began by stating that it would be about the good news concerning Jesus Christ, the Son of God. The good news is how Jesus lived and died, it is about his life and his death. That life that Jesus lived is not appealing, but challenging and inspiring. Yet the ending of the Gospel of

---

[119] Russell Pregeant, *Knowing Truth, Doing Good: Engaging New Testament Ethics* (Minneapolis, MN: Fortress Press, 2008), 148.
[120] Richard Hays, *The Moral Vision of the New Testament: A Contemporary Introduction to New Testament Ethics* (New York, NY: HarperOne, 1996), 88.

Mark skillfully narrates how everyone failed to follow
Jesus, even the three faithful women. The Gospel leaves in
our laps responsibility to *"fix the story."* We do so,
however, not by writing a happy ending, but rather by
living as followers of Jesus.

North American Christians may think they practice
discipleship in a safe zone, as Christianity is the prevailing
civil religion. Christians in first-century Palestine lived in a
more ominous context. But it is well for disciples in every
age to take note of the dramatic vocabulary of fear
throughout Mark's concluding scene. Those three women
were trying to be as faithful as they could, yet their fear
overwhelmed them. That fear may be a normal emotion for
any faithful follower of Jesus the Nazarene, the Crucified
One. Anyone who follows Jesus, taking up the cross, may
find themselves in a position that is vulnerable to potential
harm. Thus being fearful would be a realistic reaction for

any faithful follower of Jesus. I think this is something for us to consider as we continue to try to follow Jesus faithfully.

As a Korean cultural perspective indicates the male disciples did not even have the "*Jeong*" to "*stick*" by Jesus. This included the three women who were possibly doing their culturally expected funerary rituals, "*Chesa.*" Even though the three women encountered the male angelic figure in the tomb who could have been the risen Jesus, they became silent. The text invites everyone to speak and follow Jesus, even Peter, the one who denied Jesus. Maybe the original hearers of the text were comforted by it, since they may have found themselves denying Jesus as well in order to avoid persecutions or attacks. The text would have conveyed to them the good news that God, who ripped the heavens apart at the beginning of the Gospel, is on the loose again in the world, for the stone was rolled back and

Jesus was raised and is on the move again to meet with his people.

The ending of the Gospel of Mark has an open ending that points the readers to a new beginning. They are directed back to the beginning of the story, back to Galilee, to begin again the quest to follow Jesus faithfully. There are no heroes among Jesus' followers.[121] Everyone failed. Many times we, too, may remain silent when we should be speaking, testifying to the good news of Jesus Christ, the Son of God (1:1). The good news is that none of us can wander too far away from God's healing presence. But like the three women, we are summoned to speak. The text cries out for readers to act, and leaves them with a decision to make.

---

[121] Perkins, 733.

Bibliography

Anderson, Janice Capel, Stephen D. Moore. *Mark and Method*. Minneapolis, MN: Fortress Press, 2008.

Beavis, Mary Ann. *Mark*, Paideia. Grand Rapids, MI: Baker Academic, 2011.

Blount, Brian. *Cultural Interpretation: Reorienting New Testament Criticism*. Eugene, OR: Wipf and Stock Publishers, 1995.

Blount, Brian. *Go Preach!*. Maryknoll, NY: Orbis Books, 1998.

Blount, Brain. *Then the Whisper Put on Flesh: New Testament Ethics in an African American Context*. Nashville, TN: Abingdon Press, 2001.

Boring, M. Eugene. *Mark*, The New Testament Library.
Louisville, KY: Westminster John Knox Press,
2006.

Boring, M. Eugene, Fred B. Craddock. *The People's New
Testament Commentary*. Louisville, KY:
Westminster John Knox Press, 2009.

Brock, Rita Nakashima, Jung Ha Kim, Kwok Pui-Lan, and
Seung Ai Yang. *Off the Menu: Asian and Asian
North American Women's Religion & Theology*.
Louisville, KY: Westminster John Knox Press,
2007.

Carson, D.A, R.T. France, J.A. Motyer, and G.J. Wenham.
New Bible Commentary: 21st century edition.
Nottingham, England: Inter-Varsity Press, 1994.

Collins, Adela Yarbro. *Mark: A Commentary*, Hermeneia.
Minneapolis, MN: Fortress Press, 2007.

Corley, Kathleen E. *Maranatha: Women's Funerary Rituals and Christian Origins*. Minneapolis, MN: Fortress Press, 2010.

Culpepper, R. Alan. *Mark*, Smyth & Helwys Bible Commentary. Macon, GA: Smyth & Helwys Publishing, 2007.

deSilva, David A. *Honor, Patronage, Kinship & Purity: Unlocking New Testament Culture*. Downers Grove, IL: Inter Varsity Press, 2000.

Donahue, John R., Daniel J. Harrington, *The Gospel of Mark*, Sacra Pagina Series. Collegeville, MN: The Liturgical Press, 2002.

Duran, Nicole Wilkinson, Teresa Okure, and Daniel M. Patte. *Mark*, Texts@Contexts. Minneapolis, MN: Fortress Press, 2011.

Evans, Craig A. *Mark 8:27-16:20*, Word Biblical

Commentary. Nashville, TN: Thomas Nelson

Publishers, 2001.

Eum, Terry K. *Kata Markon*. North Charleston, SC:

CreateSpace, 2015

Gaventa, Beverly Roberts, Patrick D. Miller. *The Ending of*

Mark and the Ends of God. Louisville, KY:

Westminster John Knox Press, 2005

Hays, Richard. *The Moral Vision of the New Testament: A*

Contemporary Introduction to New Testament

Ethics. Minneapolis, MN: Fortress Press, 1996.

Horsley, Richard A. *Hearing the Whole Story*. Louisville,

KY: Westminster John Knox Press, 2001.

Iverson, Kelly R., Christopher W. Skinner. *Mark as Story:*

Retrospect and Prospect. Atlanta, GA: Society of

Biblical Literature, 2011.

Kim, Chongho. *Korean Shamanism: The Cultural Paradox.*
Hants, England: Ashgate, 2003.

Lane, William L. *The Gospel of Mark*, NICNT .Grand
Rapids, MI: William B. Eerdmans Publishing
Company, 1974.

Malina, Bruce J. *The New Testament World: Insights from
Cultural Anthropology.* (Louisville, KY:
Westminster John Knox Press, 2001.

Marcus, Joel. *Mark 8-16*, The Anchor Yale Bible.
Binghamton, NY: Yale University Press, 2009.

Myers, Ched. *Binding The Strong Man: A Political
Reading of Mark's Story of Jesus.* Maryknoll,
NY: Orbis Books, 1988.

Newsome, Carol A., Sharon H. Ringe, eds. *Women's Bible
Commentary.* Louisville, KY: Westminster John
Knox Press, 1998.

Newsom, Carol A., Sharon H. Ringe., and Jacqueline E.

Lapsley, eds. *Women's Bible Commentary:*

Twentieth – Anniversary Edition. Louisville, KY:

Westminster John Knox Press, 2012.

Neyrey, Jerome H. *Honor and Shame in the Gospel of*

Matthew. Louisville, KY: Westminster John Knox

Press, 1998.

Perkins, Pheme. *The Gospel of Mark*, The New

Interpreter's Bible vol. VIII. Nashville, TN:

Abingdon Press, 1994.

Powell, Mark Allan. *Fortress Introduction to the Gospels*.

Minneapolis, MN: Fortress Press, 1998.

Pregeant, Russell. *Knowing Truth, Doing Good: Engaging*

New Testament Ethics. Minneapolis, MN: Fortress

Press, 1989.

Rhoads, David, Joanna Dewey, Donald Michie. *Mark as*

Story 2nd ed. Minneapolis, MN: Fortress Press, 1999.

Rohrbaugh, Richard L. *The Social Sciences and New*

Testament Interpretation. Grand Rapids,   MI: Baker

Academic, 1996.

Tolbert, Mary Ann. *Sowing the Gospel: Mark's World in*

Literary – Historical Perspective. Minneapolis, MN:

Fortress Press, 1989.

Williamson Jr., Lamar. *Mark*, Interpretation. Louisville,

KY: John Knox Press, 1983.

Index of Ancient and Biblical References

Made in the USA
Coppell, TX
24 September 2021